D0518820

chill

chill

100 tips to relax

Jenny Sutcliffe

MQP

Published by **MQ Publications Limited**
12 The Ivories, 6–8 Northampton Street
London N1 2HY
Tel: +44 (0) 20 7359 2244
Fax:+44 (0) 20 7359 1616
email: mail@mqpublications.com
website: www.mqpublications.com

Copyright © MQ Publications Limited 2003

Text: **Copyright © 2003 Jenny Sutcliffe**
Design: **Balley Design Associates**
Series Editor: **Yvonne Deutch**

ISBN: 1-84072-521-4

10 9 8 7 6 5 4 3 2

Printed and bound in China

contents

introduction

Your head feels tight…your pulse is racing…aches and pains are starting to nag…you can almost feel your blood pressure rising. Soon, something will snap. That means it's time to chill—and this little book shows you how.

CHILL offers you 100 tried and tested ways of chilling out. Some are quick and easy, and others take just a little bit more effort—but they all work. That's because the majority of them are underpinned by hard science. Some require something of a leap of faith, but it's surprising how effective a technique can be if you make yourself believe in it.

Choose the chills that work for you. You can put your mind to work to release feel-good, anti-stress hormones, or take a more physical approach with a body chill. You may decide to adjust your personal space and use smell, color, and even a potted plant to maximize relaxation. You may find that a mood-enhancing food chill works for you, or, if you prefer, harness your body's own de-stressing powers with an energy chill. Whatever the cause of your stress, here, in *CHILL*, you'll find a way to defeat it.

mind chills

1 Memory chill

Transform your mood with a relaxing memory chill. Remember that long, lazy day on the beach? Or the sunlight glinting through the trees on a crisp winter's morning? Your brain picks up on the associations of good memories like these and triggers the release of feel-good, anti-stress hormones. So, write down a few of your favorite memories, and concentrate on each one for ten seconds: the warmth of the sun on your back, for example, reading a book by the fire, or just the sound of silence.

2 Float chill

Imagine letting your mind wander where it will, as you lie in the warm, dark embrace of a comforting cocoon of water. Sounds good? Then flotation therapy is the chill for you. Many health clubs and private clinics have flotation tanks, where you can enjoy total relaxation. Doctors agree that the therapy actively reduces stress.

And you can usually chill out even more by asking to have your favorite music piped into the tank.

Sheer bliss.

3 Laughing chill

"Laughter's the best medicine" as the old
saying goes. And, according to America's
prestigious Mayo Clinic, it's really true—the
clinic has found that having a good laugh is
like "internal jogging." Laughter releases a wave of feel-good
brain chemicals, shuts down the production of stress hormones,
boosts the immune system, and protects the heart. So make a
positive effort to look at the funny side of life. You could carry a
book of jokes around with you and dip into it at times of stress.

4 Talking chill

When you're stressed, you talk more rapidly. It's partly because
thoughts tend to whirl around in your head, and you feel there
are just too many emotions and problems to express. The
trouble is that talking quickly demands short, sharp breaths. This

raises your blood
pressure and pushes your
stress levels even higher.
The answer is to make a conscious
effort to speak more slowly when
stress strikes. You'll lower your blood
pressure and breathe deeply and
slowly. This floods your brain with
more oxygen, so that you can think
clearly and coolly, and reason your
stress away.

5 Mindless chill

Sometimes your head becomes so full of stressful thoughts and problems, you feel you might explode. That's when you need to empty your mind. One trick is to concentrate on something simple, mindless, and repetitive. Try making a paper-clip snake, building a tower of playing cards, or making a paper airplane. By the time you've finished, your subconscious mind will have had a chance to reorder your thoughts and restore your equilibrium. And you'll also have something fun to play with.

6 Praise chill

Personal slights and setbacks make it hard to feel relaxed and at ease with yourself. When you find yourself stressed by random injustices, or unkindness from others, calm yourself with a praise chill. Make a list of your good points: note your finest qualities and your best achievements—and write them down on cards for easy reference. Then you can run through them when things start getting on top of you. Simply increasing your self-esteem, and drawing on positive associations, will quickly bring you back onto an even keel.

7 Smile chill

Contentment and pleasure make you smile—that's obvious. But less obviously, the very act of smiling can relax you and make you feel good. This is because your brain recognizes the pattern of muscular contractions that shape your mouth into a smile. First, it looks for something to be pleased about—a picture on your desk, say. Then it reinforces the contractions, intensifying the smile and raising the pleasure stakes. Try it for yourself—you'll be pleasantly surprised at how effective it is. So, from now on, when things are getting really tense, just smile, and fool your brain into a state of chilled contentment.

8 Pet chill

A University of California study reports that people who own dogs suffer from stress significantly less than those who don't. And it's not just dogs that provide a chill factor: any pet has the same effect—even watching a tank full of fish for a few minutes has been shown to reduce stress levels. Get yourself beautifully chilled by stroking and cuddling your pet whenever you're stressed. And if you don't have a pet of your own, make friends with someone else's. Take a neighbor's dog for a walk regularly, and you'll soon be receiving warm, unconditional love—as well as the feel-good effects of all that extra exercise.

9 Whistle chill

Nobody knows why whistling relaxes you, but it does the trick. Perhaps it's for the same reason that laughing or smiling works: the brain is nudged into thinking that there's a reason to laugh or smile. Certainly, you often find yourself whistling away when you're happy. So just whistle a happy tune and chill out.

10 Tone chill

If you find it hard to release your pent-up emotions, unexpressed feelings can become a major source of stress. The art of "toning" could be the answer. You can learn the technique from a toning therapist, or just experiment on your own. Find yourself some peace and quiet and then "sing" using a variety of basic sounds: yell, screech, grunt, and hum. With practice, you'll start to feel which sounds are the right ones for you, and relax as all those hidden fears and worries leave your mind.

19

11 Hypno chill

We don't have to fight saber-toothed tigers nowadays, but we still have the same "fight-or-flight" response to threats as our ancestors—a big adrenaline rush. A succession of the most trivial nuisances can lead to a stressful build-up of adrenaline. When this happens, you can clear it from your system by using mild self-hypnosis techniques known as autogenic training. Ideally, you should sign up for a course, but you can start by spending ten minutes focusing on sensations of warmth and heaviness in each part of your body in turn. You'll feel your tension float away.

12 Burn chill

Ever sent a lethal letter
demonstrating that you're right,
and the other person is wrong? Remember
the feeling of satisfaction you had afterward? You felt
so much better, didn't you? So, next time you're angry
with someone, write a cutting letter saying what's upsetting you.
Then burn it, and feel the chill as the stress goes up in smoke.

13 Pulse chill

Biofeedback equipment has proved that your mind can control
bodily functions. That means you can learn to will stress away. You
don't even need equipment. Just find your pulse, and concentrate
on slowing it—it helps to intone "slower," "slower," "slower" as
you focus. It takes practice, but soon you'll be able to control
your pulse rate and reduce your stress levels wherever you are.

14 Walk away chill

The more negative emotions you carry around with you, the more stressed you become. This is because emotions can be transmitted from person to person as easily as a cold. Your subconscious immediately recognizes someone else's bad mood and starts to generate its own negative reactions. And these can quickly build up and flood your mind, making you tense and depressed.

When this happens to you, deal with the problem quickly and effectively. Make a conscious decision to walk away from tense situations with a spring in your step, and stay chilled, relaxed, and positive.

15 Fantasy chill

What do you really, really want? Success in your career? A committed relationship? A big win in the lottery? Everybody dreams about something, so use your dreams to get an instant chill. Construct the fantasy of your choice and work it out in detail. For instance, if you long for a new house, plan its ground plan thoroughly. Then, when life gets too much, you can walk through your house room by room, and work out where you want to place the furniture, and what color you will paint the walls. By the end of your dream tour, life will be looking rosy again.

16 Perspective chill

When you're stressed, little things take on an importance out of all proportion to their real significance. If you ask yourself "Will this matter in a year's time?" the answer will be "no" nine times out of ten. So, take a long, hard look at how important your problem really is. After you've dismissed all the minor problems you'll be able to think clearly about the important ones.

17 Auto chill

"Every day, in every way, I am getting better and better," was the mantra of Emile Coué, the father of autosuggestion. And his technique has been shown to be a highly effective stress buster. Positive suggestions can be implanted into your mind and regular reinforcement persuades the subconscious to act on them. So make up a positive phrase—it could be as simple as "I feel relaxed and peaceful," and repeat it to yourself at times of stress.

18 Doodle chill

Sometimes you just can't see the solution to a problem. The trouble is that you're overworking the logical left side of your brain. Break out of the pattern by doodling. This uses the more creative, artistic right side of your brain and rests the left brain. It also opens up the connections between the two sides, enabling a flash of right-sided inspiration to throw light on the problem.

19 Book chill

Reading can be a great way to distract you from stress by taking you into a world of illusion. But it doesn't necessarily reduce your stress levels—especially when the book is a suspense-filled thriller, and you don't know what's going to happen. The secret of a successful book chill is to make sure that there aren't any nasty surprises. So curl up in front of the fire and reread one of your favorite books—preferably one that has a happy ending.

20 Perfect day chill

Positive thinking is an effective way of reducing stress levels, but positive writing is even more effective. That's probably because the very activity of writing implants the beneficial associations in more extensive areas of the brain. When you're stressed, write a story—about your perfect day, perhaps. But keep it to no more than 25 words—brevity demands clarity and adds resonance. You might start off with "Shower. Tea and toast. Newspaper. Laze…" and go from there.

body chills

21 Blink chill

If you spend all day looking at a computer screen, there's a fair
chance that you suffer to some degree from what's now called
"computer vision syndrome." Its symptoms are eye irritation and
fatigue, headaches, backaches, and muscle spasms—in short,
stress. It's important to have your eyes tested regularly and to
take frequent breaks, of course, but you can also reduce stress
with a blink chill. Simply blink every so often to lubricate your
eyes and keep them from drying out. Otherwise, splash water
into them, or lie back with your eyes covered in cool, refreshing
cucumber slices.

22 Tension chill

Physical tension sits in your neck and shoulders, as if you're
carrying a heavy weight on your back. Relieve the pressure every
hour or so with this quick tension chill. Knead your neck muscles

using small, but firm, circling movements with your fingertips. Go right up to the skull bone but not beneath it—stop at once if you start to feel dizzy. Then work slowly along the muscles running from the base of your neck to each shoulder, and feel the tension drain away.

23 Punch chill

In India, attending martial arts classes is considered a stress management technique; and in some Chinese prisons, inmates are given sandbags so that they can punch their stress away. You probably know how it feels to want to hit someone or something when you're stressed out. Buy one of the many executive stress busting toys on the market, or simply blow up a few balloons and tie them to a table with some string. Then punch away to your heart's content—this will work out all your aggression and reduce your stress levels.

24 Wet chill

Dehydration not only affects concentration but leads to physical stress. Every day, you need to drink at least eight to ten 8oz glasses of water to avoid becoming dehydrated. And that's before you take into account the effects of the warm, dry air in most offices, and your intake of tea, coffee, and alcohol, all of which cause you to lose water from your body. So, take a water chill. Make sure that there's a bottle of water at hand wherever you are, and take regular drinks throughout the day. You'll be surprised at how much more alert you feel.

25 Nap chill

As the morning wears on, your performance levels start to fall and stress levels begin to increase, as "burnout" sets in. Harvard University researchers have shown that this happens because your visual circuits become overloaded with information. But they've also shown that taking a lunchtime nap reverses the burnout process. Make it part of your routine to close your eyes and relax for half-an-hour. It doesn't matter whether or not you fall asleep—the main thing is that you give your brain time to process and assimilate all of the morning's information.

26 Reflex chill

You may not think that reflexology has any direct medical value, and all the serious scientific studies would agree with you. But thousands of people also agree that a foot massage is incredibly relaxing—not just for your feet, but for the whole body. It's easy to see why the 26 bones, 3 main arches, and more than 100 ligaments that make up each foot might need to be relieved of stress. After all, your feet have to bear the whole weight of your body, and are often encased in constricting fashion shoes. It's certainly worth a try.

27 Breathe chill

Most of us only use about half our lung capacity, which means that carbon dioxide builds up in our bodies, and insufficient oxygen is taken in. The problem is that too much CO_2 raises your heart rate and prevents clear thinking—and that means stress. The remedy is a breathe chill. Place your hands on your lower ribs, with your fingers touching in the middle. Breathe in deeply and slowly, feeling your ribs move up and apart as your stomach rises. Hold for a count of three, then breathe out. Repeat four times and feel the oxygen relieve your stress.

28 One-legged chill

It sounds unlikely, agreed. But there are sound neurological reasons why standing on one leg for a few moments is relaxing. When you're standing on one leg, your brain has to analyze a huge number of sensory inputs from your muscles, and relate them to your position in three dimensions. Then it has to send motor signals to the muscles to make the constant adjustments needed to keep your balance. The effect is to integrate your physical body and mind, and to inhibit any other stimuli. It's like giving your brain a spring cleaning. So, try a one-legged chill.

29 Achievement chill

There are always jobs that you haven't
got around to doing, both at work and at home, and it's
surprising how virtuous and pleased with yourself you feel when
you complete one. In fact, it's an achievement chill. Part of the
effect, of course, comes from the fact that concentrating on
mundane task distracts you from more serious worries. But
there's also the sheer satisfaction of finishing a job, when it may
be the only task you've managed to complete successfully during
your day. Fix that leaking faucet now, and give yourself an
achievement chill.

30 Relax chill

Mental relaxation and physical relaxation are inextricably linked. So, relax your body progressively, and your mind will follow. Lie flat on your back, let your mind go blank, and take a few deep breaths. Start with your left toes: tense the muscles, hold, and then "let go," making them feel floppy, heavy, and warm—it takes practice. Then use the same technique on all the muscle groups of your left leg, before working on your right leg. Next, move up your body, finishing with your head, neck, and mouth. Finally, just breathe deeply and sigh your tensions away.

31 Emergency chill

Nobody knows why, but sometimes extreme stress or anxiety makes you hyperventilate: your breathing suddenly becomes rapid, shallow, and forced—this is what's commonly called a panic attack. The result is a dangerous imbalance between CO_2 and O_2 levels: too much CO_2 is breathed out and too little O_2 is taken in. If you feel a panic attack coming on, you can try the Breathe chill (page 35). But to combat a full-blown panic attack, you'll have to take a different approach. You need to use a small paper bag. Place this over your nose and mouth, and breathe in and out four or five times to balance out the levels. In a little while you'll find that the feelings of panic have subsided.

32 Bead chill

When a dog is torn between taking one course of action or another it usually takes neither. Instead, it does something that is both completely different and trivial—it sits down and scratches, for example. The dog is carrying out a displacement activity. It's occupying its conscious mind with an external stimulus, while its subconscious mind solves the problem. You can do the same. Get some worry beads, and focus on repeating movements and routines while you play with them. Soon, your subconscious will have reordered your mind, and taken your worries away.

33 Chill chill

A tension headache can be misery. There's a dull thudding inside your temples and your brain feels as if it's about to explode. Of course, you could just take an aspirin—but a much faster, and equally effective, remedy is a chill chill. If you're in an office, just soak a cloth in some water from the cooler, then close your eyes and hold it firmly against your forehead for five or ten minutes. At home, wrap a packet of frozen peas in a dish towel and do the same. In a short while you'll be back to normal.

34 Spa chill

Sometimes there's just no substitute for self-indulgent hedonism when your stress levels reach the ceiling and you're desperate to relax. That's when it's time to take a spa chill. Visit your nearest health club, and spend an afternoon—or even a day—being toned and pampered. Have a massage, cover yourself in mud, revel in sitz baths and jacuzzis, take some gentle exercise, and indulge yourself with some beauty treatments. Make up your mind to be a king or queen for a day, and wallow in a world of carefree cosseting. It'll make the real world seem an altogether more relaxing place.

35 Postural chill

"Walk tall!" your parents used to say.
And they were right. Bad posture puts
all sorts of strains on your muscles and ligaments,
as they fight to compensate for an unnatural
position, which leads to physical and mental tension.
The solution is to give yourself a postural chill.
Stand in front of a mirror: put your shoulders
back, but not too rigidly; tuck your
bottom in; and make sure your
head is in the same plane as
your pelvis and that its crown
is your highest part. Practice
correct posture until it is
natural—and enjoy the
extra self-confidence
you'll feel.

36 Massage chill

When you want to comfort somebody, you hug them
—it's all part of the basic human need to touch and be touched.
Therapeutic massage draws on this principle for just one of its
benefits. But it also relieves muscle tension, improves blood
circulation and the disposal of toxins, and calms and soothes the
nervous system, giving an overall sense of well-being. So, if you're
feeling stressed, book a session with a qualified masseur—after
all, you take your car in for a service, so why not your body?
You'll end up feeling toned yet relaxed and, above all, positive
about life.

37 Bath chill

A long, hot soak does wonders for both mind and body. The heat helps relax knotted, tense muscles, while water supports some of your body weight and laps you with comfort. It's probably the cheapest, easiest, and most self-indulgent way of chilling—and it's even better if you add some aromatic oil to the water. So when it's been a long, hard day, unplug the phone and take a bath chill. Make sure the bathroom's warm, have a good book at hand—and perhaps a glass of wine—and just lie back into the warmth and peace. Magic.

38 Sling chill

A sunny afternoon, a shady spot, a good book, and…
a hammock. Supported completely, you just lie back in
mid-air, rock gently to and fro, and take it easy. There's nothing
better. Some researchers think that lying in a hammock is relaxing
because your subconscious picks up on how similar the
experience is to being back in the womb. The hammock
supports you in space, just like amniotic fluid, while the rocking
mimics the way you reacted to your mother's movements.
But whatever the reason, it works, so relax into a sling chill.

39 Evolutionary chill

Nobody knows why, but when you take exercise, your brain releases opiate, feel-good chemicals called endorphins that reduce stress. Unfortunately, if you overdo exercise, you can feel not just good, but euphoric, and that feeling can be addictive—it's the "runner's high." The answer is to take a controlled amount of exercise regularly. Professor Art de Vany promotes "evolutionary fitness," which mirrors the activity patterns of our hunter-gatherer ancestors. You do two, 40-minute intense workouts a week and one longer session of less intense activity, such as brisk walking or jogging, to blow your mental cobwebs away.

40 Vision chill

Picture a hunter in the forest: still, calm, aware of everything around, but alert and ready to pounce. The hunter is using peripheral vision, scanning a whole panorama of the area. The stillness and calmness is because, unlike normal vision, peripheral vision is linked to brain centers associated with relaxation. You can learn how to tune into these centers by switching to peripheral vision for a few moments. Look straight ahead and stretch one hand out to your side until you can only see it if you move your fingers. Then concentrate on sensing what's behind it for a relaxing peripheral chill.

space chills

41 Plant chill

Modern offices are full of toxic vapors: formaldehyde, for example, used in the manufacture of office furniture; and benzene, used in cleaning materials. They are thought to be the cause of what's become known as "sick building syndrome." But now you can do something about it, and chill your workspace. A two-year study by NASA showed that potted plants can filter the toxins out of your working environment. So, put a plant on your desk—it can be a flowering variety or a simple green plant.

42 Light chill

They call it the "winter blues"—the feeling of listlessness and depression that can dog the short days and long nights of winter. But you can easily recapture that summertime feeling with a light chill. Buy a light box or light visor—try health stores or the

Internet—and
spend 30
minutes a day
basking in the
life-enhancing rays.
You'll soon reset
your internal clock
to summertime, and this
chases the blues away. As an
additional benefit, the light
can help to clear up any
skin problems, too.

43 Ion chill

Think of the feeling of freshness that follows a quick shower, or how invigorating it can be to stand beside a waterfall. It's all down to negative ions. Ions are electrically charged particles in the air we breathe. If the charge is positive—when it's "close" before a thunderstorm, for example—you tend to feel lethargic and irritable. But when negative ions are around, as in the air near running water, your mood becomes more positive. Nowadays you don't need to find a waterfall to change your mood. Just buy a small ioniser and recharge your home or office.

44 Tidy chill

The last thing you need when you're stressed is the hassle of irritating distractions. It's all too easy to raise your emotional temperature if you have to search for that file you've mislaid or go through a mass of papers to find one important document.

The answer is to make a regular, preemptive strike on disorganization—a tidy chill. It's boring but it works. Look around your home or office: what don't you need and what can you throw away? What do you need and is it easily accessible? De-clutter your environment and you'll de-clutter your mind.

45 Music chill

Music therapy has long been an established branch of psychotherapy, especially when it comes to treating depression, stress, and emotional problems. And a little DIY music therapy is a great way of giving yourself a quick music chill. But there are some rules. Rock, for example, can give you the reverse of a chill, because the typical rock beat can increase stress. And the response to classical music can vary according to the composer and the work. Instead, try the more flowing rhythms of jazz or blues for a quick uplift of your spirits.

46 Color chill

It's been known for a long time that
colors affect your mood. Red, orange, and
yellow stimulate the appetite, for example—
that's why they're so often used in fast-food
restaurant decor. Conversely, blue shades calm you and lower
your blood pressure, while green tones
relax you mentally as well as
physically and help guard
against depression. So, choose
chill tones when you plan
your home's color scheme,
and give yourself a head
start when it comes to
total relaxation.

47 Ergo chill

"Ergo" stands for ergonomics—the science of designing a working environment for maximum comfort and efficiency. And when it comes to working with computers, good ergonomics is essential, if you're to avoid unnecessary stress. Do your hands fall naturally on the keyboard with your forearms supported, by armrests if necessary? Are you looking directly at your VDU, rather than down at it? And is your chair comfortable, adjustable, and one that supports your lower back? If you answer "no" to any of these questions, it's time to take action and give your workstation an ergo chill.

48 Vanilla chill

Since the early 1990s, perfume makers have been incorporating vanilla into their scents. Why? Because several medical research studies of the time showed that the smell of vanilla calms you by inhibiting your "startle-reflex" and reduces stress and anxiety. But you don't have to buy expensive perfumes to experience a vanilla chill. In fact, the chill is more pronounced when vanilla is in its pure state. Just buy a small bottle of pure vanilla essence, and dribble a few drops onto a handkerchief—ready to calm yourself down whenever things get on top of you.

49 Daylight chill

The light that you get from most artificial light sources has a reddish, yellowish tinge and doesn't contain the full color spectrum of natural daylight. And research has shown that constant exposure to artificial light not only causes eyestrain, but also increases stress by reducing emotional well-being. If this problem rings a bell with you, try a daylight chill. Simply replace the regular light bulb in the lamp on your desk with a full-spectrum natural daylight one. It will be more expensive, but the reduction in your stress levels will certainly be worth the price.

50 Humid chill

Are your lips and skin chapped? Do your nose and throat feel dry and scratchy? Is your chest tight and is your breathing becoming difficult? If so, you probably need a humid chill. Too little humidity causes stress, so buy a hygrometer from your local hardware store and check the humidity in your home or workplace: it should be between 40 and 50 percent. If there's a problem, you can solve it quickly and easily. Buy yourself a humidifier—or simply put a bowl of water by a radiator—and you'll soon notice the difference.

51 Silence chill

According to the World Health Organization, the acceptable level of noise is 45 decibels—exposure to anything above that over long periods can cause stress, and, in extreme cases, permanent hearing loss. But normal conversation is rated at 40dbs, while a ringing phone is 60 dbs. When you're surrounded by noise and are beginning to feel stressed, you probably need a silence chill. Ask for soundproof partitions to be installed in your office, turn off any noisy appliances, and buy yourself some earplugs if all else fails.

52 Haven chill

It's a deep-rooted human instinct to find a safe haven—somewhere warm and cozy, where dangers and hidden fears can't penetrate, and you can relax completely, surrounded by your familiar things. Why not take advantage of the chill that this instinct brings. Create your private haven: a familiar chair in front of the fire, perhaps, with photographs of family and friends at hand, a glass of wine, and your favorite magazine. Spend ten minutes or so there when you come home from work, enjoying the peace, quiet, and security of a haven chill.

53 Road chill

Road rage is a defining phenomena of the modern age. And it's hardly conducive to relaxation. You can't do much about somebody else's road rage, but you can make it less likely that you'll succumb. Make your car a place of calm: fill it with a pleasing fragrance, play relaxing music, make sure it's neither too warm nor too cold. Look after your own comfort, too: wear loose clothes and support your lower spine with a lumbar pad. Then you can chill out when those road hogs cut you off.

54 Bedroom chill

Bedrooms may score low on our list of priorities for attention. That's a pity, because it's vital to get enough sleep if you want to stay relaxed and focused during the day—and it's much more difficult to sleep well if your bedroom is a cold, unwelcoming, untidy place. So, give your sleeping space a calming chill.

Decorate it in calming, de-stressing colors—warm blues are ideal—and check your mattress and bed linen for warmth and comfort. And don't forget to put away those piles of clothes. You'll find that you wake up in the morning happy and chilled.

55 Cool chill

Airline pilots have to stay alert, relaxed, and operating at maximum efficiency. One way that airlines achieve this is by making sure that the cockpit temperature doesn't rise too much. The reason is that your body and mind just don't work efficiently if it's too warm—as that creates stress. In fact, efficiency is believed to drop by 15 percent if the temperature rises to 75°F/24°C. So check the room temperature if your stress levels rise, turn down the heating, and take a cool chill—the World Health Organization recommends that the optimum office temperature is 60.8°F/16°C.

56 Nature chill

After a while, you don't even notice the noises, the smells, and the incessant hustle and bustle of city life. But your body is aware of the pollution, the constant sense of threat, and the sensory overload of urban living, and responds by increasing your stress levels. The answer is to take a step back and try a nature chill. Get out of town and just wallow in the peace and quiet of the open countryside, breathing in fresh, pure air and relaxing into the unhurried tranquillity of the natural world.

57 Info chill

Information overload is a fact of modern working life. Sometimes there seems to be hardly enough time in the day to read your e-mails, let alone organize your diary. And it can be highly stressful to feel that you're not on top of things. When the load becomes too much, you need an info chill. Take the phone off the

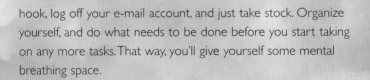

hook, log off your e-mail account, and just take stock. Organize yourself, and do what needs to be done before you start taking on any more tasks. That way, you'll give yourself some mental breathing space.

58 Joss chill

For centuries, people have raised their spirits and driven away stress by burning incense. For example, Buddhists burn it to rid themselves of negativity and increase self-awareness. Ancient Sanskrit texts describe how incense uplifts the mind and fills the heart with euphoria; and Egypt's pharaohs used incense to drive away evil spirits and attract the gods. You can try a joss-stick chill when you're feeling down. Choose warm, earthy patchouli, a spring-like strawberry fragrance, soothing jasmine, or piquant sandalwood. Then watch your troubles drift away on tendrils of smoke.

59 Ambience chill

When the narrator of Proust's *À la Recherche de Temps Perdu* (*Remembrance of Things Past*) smells a small cake called a *madeleine*, he's transported back to the world of his childhood. It's not surprising, because the sense of smell, uniquely, passes directly into the brain's emotional centers. And smells don't just trigger happy associations: they can also change your mood. London's subways have used a rose and jasmine aroma—known as "Madeleine"—to soothe weary travelers; and, in Japan, jasmine and camomile are piped through offices to aid relaxation. So, fill your living space with the fragrances that trigger your chill.

60 Clothes chill

The fashion for office "dress-down" days may be on the wane, but it's still important that you feel relaxed in your clothes— they're your immediate personal environment. It doesn't help you relax if you look good, but feel uncomfortable. Take a fashion chill instead of being a fashion victim. Make sure that your clothes are loose fitting and allow you to feel at ease; also, pay particular attention to wearing the right shoes—they don't have to be "sensible," just well-fitting. And avoid high heels, because these can cause severe and stressful pain in your lower back.

food chills

61 Camomile chill

Anxiety and stress don't make for a good night's sleep, and lack of sleep creates more stress. It's a vicious circle. Break it with a bedtime cup of calming camomile tea—in some old herbals, camomile is called "nervine" because of its tranquilizing effect on the nervous system. You can buy camomile teabags from health shops, but pick and home-dry your own flowers for maximum flavor and benefit. Then savor the tea's light, apple-like fragrance as you're gently soothed into untroubled sleep.

62 Nut chill

Finding it hard to concentrate? Lacking energy? Stressed and depressed, especially when you're suffering the after-effects of the night before? Try nuts—a handful of them. Bite into a few Brazil nuts, nibble on an almond or two, and within minutes you'll feel your spirits rise and your sense of purpose grow. Brazil nuts contain the mood-enhancing mineral selenium, while almonds are a rich source of magnesium. Reduced levels of either of these in the brain have been linked to depression, irritability, and mood swings. And it's also worth remembering that drinking too much lowers your magnesium levels.

63 Carb chill

Proteins, such as meat, fish, and dairy products, contain tyrosine, a chemical that is converted into neurotransmitters in the brain—so they make you more alert. That's fine, but sometimes you don't want to be alert and ready for anything: you just want to chill. That's when you need a carb chill. Eat a helping of carbohydrates, such as pasta, bread, rice, or potatoes, and you'll increase the levels of calming, relaxing serotonin in your brain. Soon you'll feel more sleepy—almost sluggish—your stress is lifted and your reaction times slow.

64 Juice chill

According to researchers at the University of Alabama-Huntsville, large doses of Vitamin C stopped the production of stress hormones in rats. But we're not rats, and for some people, megadoses of Vitamin C can be dangerous. Even so, it's worthwhile taking a juice chill. Just an 8oz glass of fresh, unadulterated orange juice provides more than enough Vitamin C to meet the recommended daily allowance—and it's completely natural. Make a glass of orange juice part of your breakfast routine and cut down your stress hormone levels.

65 Herbal chill

Most people kick start their day with a cup of tea or coffee—in other words, with a slug of caffeine. The problem is that a caffeine jolt works because it triggers the production of adrenaline, the "fight-or-flight" stress hormone. And more cups of coffee or tea just keep your stress levels high. But there is an alternative: a herbal chill. Instead of topping up on caffeine all day, try a fragrant glass of herbal tea—but make sure it's a true, caffeine-free tea. Then your adrenaline levels will drop during your day rather than rise.

66 Passion chill

Unfortunately, it's not that type of passion. Instead, it's the exotic passionflower, which opens for just one day, and reminded the missionaries who discovered it of the sufferings of Jesus on the Cross. Passionflower is a fascinating plant, and has remarkable and well-attested properties. It's a natural painkiller that acts against anxiety and nervous tension to relieve stress. So give yourself a passion chill when you need to relax—it's available in capsule form or as passionflower tea (it's often combined with hawthorn berries for even greater effect.)

67 Valerian chill

Some generous people think that valerian, also known as nature's tranquilizer, has an earthy, musky scent; most, more realistically, think its odor is less glamorous, and call it "the gym-sock herb." But while you would have to be very brave to drink valerian tea, you can still take a valerian chill in pill form. As well as relieving anxiety and preventing insomnia, valerian relaxes stressed muscles—in short, it's an all-around natural sedative. But you should be careful not to overdose, and for safety only use valerian for a few days at a time.

68 Chocolate chill

Nobody quite knows why chocolate is so wonderful. Some people say it's because it's chock full of a feel-good chemical related to amphetamine that's also released when we fall in love; less romantic types say that none of the chemical actually reaches the brain and point out that chocolate contains the stimulant theobromine. But they're all missing the point. The fact is that eating chocolate just makes you feel so good—a chocolate chill really works. So just relax as it melts luxuriously in your mouth and the rich, creamy taste makes love to your taste buds.

69 Vitamin chill

When you're under stress, you deplete your body's store of essential vitamins, particularly the B group—and the lack of these vital nutrients can cause further stress. At the same time, Vitamin C is known to have anti-stress properties. So, you may benefit from a vitamin chill. In an ideal world, we'd get all the vitamins we need from a healthy balanced diet, but it's not always easy to eat properly when you're on the go. To be sure, simply take a simple multivitamin pill as part of your daily routine.

70 Banana chill

Bananas are the ultimate fast food. They're convenient, portable, self-contained, fiber-rich, fat-free (with only 100-odd calories), and packed with carbohydrates, vitamins, and minerals. They're also perfect as mood food. It's not just the calming carbohydrates that make a banana chill work. Bananas contain tryptophan, which plays a vital role in the production of the feel-good brain chemical serotonin, as well as more Vitamin B6, which stress depletes, than any other fruit. And if that's not enough, they're rich in potassium, which is vital for brain function. So, unzip a banana when you feel low.

71 Soup chill

Your mother really did know best: chicken soup works miracles. Now researchers have shown that it doesn't just clear up a cold—it's also brain food, improving memory and thought processes. Apparently it's all due to a chemical called proline, which is found in the tissues that dissolve when a carcass is boiled. So when you're cooking a chicken dinner, give yourself a soup chill. Boil up the leftovers with some herbs, stock, seasoning, and vegetables, and you'll be just an hour or so away from nourishing your mind as well as comforting your body. Enjoy.

72 Dinner chill

Sometimes the best way to chill out is to take your mind off things for a while and give your brain a chance to give itself a spring cleaning. And fine food and great wines can often be the perfect recipe. A dinner chill could be just what you need. Pick a congenial companion—and pamper both your taste buds and your mind. Of course, it needn't necessarily be expensive. All the poet Omar Khayyam needed was "A jug of wine, a loaf of bread and thou beside me singing in the wilderness..."

73 Ice cream chill

Have you ever seen anybody look stressed when they're eating ice cream? Thought not. The fact is that ice cream makes you happy, and when you're happy you relax.

Of course, it may be due to its associations with childhood: the music of the ice cream truck and the excited dash to buy a cone. But it may be because ice cream is loaded with carbohydrates, which soothe and calm you. Or, over the long term, due to ice cream's high calcium content, because calcium is used up by stress. So don't feel guilty: have an ice cream chill.

74 Diet chill

It's generally acknowledged that a good diet plays an important part in stress avoidance. And there's no shortage of advice about what constitutes a good program. The trouble is that everyone has different needs—for instance, an office worker requires a very different diet from that of somebody doing hard, physical work outdoors. And your size, shape, medical history, and metabolic rate are also significant factors. That's why it's a good idea to take a long-term diet chill. Consult a qualified dietician and work out a plan that's just right for you. Follow it and start a new, relaxed life.

75 Freeze chill

When you're stressed, your mouth and throat tighten up and hold in the tension. But a cold sensation in your mouth can release the tension—and it can help relieve tension headaches, too. In fact, women in labor are often given ice cubes to suck for this reason. So, put your stress into cold storage with a freeze chill. An ice cube is fine—or even an ice lolly—but if you're feeling that little bit decadent, try sucking on a frozen grape instead. And if you're feeling seriously decadent, you could always peel it first.

76 Magnesium chill

Nervous tension? Irritability? Cravings for sugary foods? A tendency to constipation? If these symptoms ring a bell, you may be suffering from a deficiency of magnesium, which is stored in the brain. And levels of magnesium are depleted by stress—some people call it "the stress mineral." It's simple to restore your levels with a magnesium chill. Eat magnesium-rich foods, such as apples, oats, cabbage, whole wheat, parsley, and soybeans, and cut down on high-fat foods, which also reduce how much magnesium is absorbed. And if you find that a problem, simply take a magnesium supplement every day.

77 Porridge chill

Over the past few years, scientists have started to realize that a chemical called gamma-amino butyric acid—it's easier to say "GABA"—plays a vital role in promoting mental relaxation. So much so, in fact, that the race is on to develop a whole new range of mood-stabilizing drugs based on GABA. But until they succeed, there's a simple way of upping your GABA levels—take a porridge chill. Oats are rich in GABA, and porridge is a practical, delicious, and satisfying way of taking them.

78 Caviar chill

If your problems seem insoluble and you're so stressed that you can't think straight, what you need is a caviar chill. Why? Because your memory and your ability to think clearly and quickly are controlled by your brain's cognition system—and this needs a chemical called acetylcholine to function properly. Now if you need to boost your choline levels, you could always eat more eggs or whole grains, because they're rich in cholines. But it shouldn't be too hard to persuade yourself that caviar is the most appropriate source for you. So go ahead and take a delicious caviar chill. Why not?

79 Seaweed chill

In Japan, seaweed is a staple of soups, salads, and starters; in China, it's eaten in stir-fries, rolls, and noodle dishes; in Wales, where it's called "laver bread," seaweed is fried in bacon fat and served on toast with cockles. Why? Not just because it tastes good. In a nutshell, seaweed is rich in iodine. This element is essential for the thyroid gland, which controls the body's energy levels—and stress drains iodine reserves. Replenish them and energize yourself with a seaweed chill—and if you can't face seaweed, you can always take it in pill form.

80 Comfort chill

There's something so warm, relaxing, and comforting about childhood food. Perhaps it's because the tastes and smells take you back to a world of certainties and simplicity, of warmth and security, in which the sun always shines and there's honey still for tea. Everyone has their own favorite, of course. But whether yours is boiled eggs and toast, peanut butter sandwiches, chocolate cake, hot sausage and mustard, or cold jello and custard, take yourself back to that stress-free nursery with a comfort chill. You'll be ready to handle anything when you return to the real world.

CHAPTER FIVE

Energy chills

81 Chakra chill

In yoga, the seven chakras are the body's centers of life-energy.
Each one is associated with a mantra such as "om" or "ram,"
which is chanted during meditation, and breathing exercises to
regulate the body's energy flow. If you don't have time to learn
about yoga, you can still try a chakra chill. You'll find that chanting
while controlling your breathing will lower your blood pressure
and heart rate within a few minutes. Repeat a rhyme, chant a
sonorous phrase, or simply hum to relax both body and mind.

82 Puncture chill

It's generally accepted that acupuncture relieves pain effectively,
but the jury is still out about whether it can relieve stress. The
theory is that, in good health, the body's life energy, *chi*
(pronounce it "chee"), flows smoothly through channels called
meridians. But in sickness or stress, the flow is disrupted.

Acupuncture removes energy blockages and stabilizes the body. Some people find it a very effective way of relieving stress—and you might be one of them. So consult a qualified and insured acupuncturist and try a puncture chill.

83 Playing dead chill

Even Harvard Medical School has acknowledged that yoga reduces anxiety, blood pressure, and heart rate—which means it reduces stress. And probably the simplest and most relaxing yoga position is Savasana—the corpse posture. It's just like playing dead. Lie on your back on the ground with your legs and hands apart and your palms upward, with your whole body touching the ground. Compose yourself, breathing deeply and regularly—this is *pranayama*, in which you rebalance your *prana,* or life energy. Let your muscles go in a tide of relaxation that ripples from feet to head.

84 Rescue chill

In the early 1930s, Dr. Edward Bach categorized emotions, coming up with 38 different states. Then he experimented with flowers, gauging the effect that their "auras" had on each emotional state. When he found one that changed it, he soaked it in spring water and then preserved the water in brandy to make up remedies. Perhaps the most famous of his cures is the Bach "Rescue Remedy," made up of five different flowers, spring water, and alcohol. Thousands of people take one when stress hits hard. So take a rescue chill and see if it works for you. It contains:

Star of Bethlehem for shock

Clematis for being dreamy and forgetful

Cherry Plum for fears about mental breakdown and anger

Impatiens for irritability and tension

Rock Rose for terror and fright

85 Pressure chill

Acupressure is really DIY acupuncture, but without the needles.
Instead of stimulating the acupoints directly (these are where the
meridians run near to the skin), you apply pressure to them with
your fingertips or thumb. Press down, increasing the pressure
gradually, hold for about 20 seconds, then release slowly. There
are several acupoints for general stress: apply pressure to the tip
of your thumb, or to the muscle in the corner between your
thumb and first finger. And chill a tension headache by pressing in
the hollow at the top of your nose between your eyebrows.

86 Band chill

Stressed because of memory problems or a headache? You need
a band chill—and it's really simple. Place one hand over the other
with your thumbs interlocking. At the end of the first finger of
your upper hand, you'll find a small depression on your wrist—it's

an acupoint. Put an elastic band on your wrist—not too tightly—so that it covers the point. Then, simply snap the band over the acupoint when you're in need of a chill. Have a band chill when you're thinking negative thoughts, too—it's a great way of snapping yourself out of them.

87 Think chill

Sometimes you just need to switch off for while to give your brain time to organize itself, though it's easier said than done. But you can help yourself stop the clock by adapting meditation techniques in a think chill. Get yourself comfortable, then choose a small object—for instance, a flower, a stone, or a crystal—breathe deeply, and concentrate on it. Sense its smell, its shape, and its texture. Focus all your energy on your chosen object and pull yourself back to it if your mind wanders. After ten minutes or so, you'll be relaxed and ready for the fray once more.

88 Crystal chill

A common thread runs through the cultures of Native Americans, the Inuit, Tibetans, and the Amazonian Indians: the belief that crystals store "life energy" that can be used for healing. And today's crystal therapists are rediscovering some of this ancient knowledge. Amethyst is said to bring peace of mind, and rose quartz is acclaimed as the most effective stress reliever. Many therapists say that you shouldn't choose the crystal, but let it choose you. Hold it in your hand and visualize its vibrations when you're stressed, or wear it as a necklace next to your skin for a permanent crystal chill.

89 Healing chill

Many alternative therapists believe that we all have the potential to heal ourselves by tapping into the body's natural healing energy. So, take a healing chill to relieve your stress. Sitting comfortably, place your hands a few inches apart in the prayer position—concentrate and you may feel a slight pull between them. After a few moments, place your hands on either side of your head, with the heels of your hands touching your earlobes. Sense the energy flowing between them as your tension eases. Then return to the prayer position and rest quietly for a while.

90 Wind and water chill

Feng shui literally means "wind and water"—and its trained practitioners manipulate *chi* (life energy) so that it moves freely through space to promote health, harmony, and relaxation. You can only be sure of a healthy, harmonious environment if you consult a feng shui expert. But there are some simple ways of giving your space a wind and water chill: remove all clutter; use mirrors with care, as they can disrupt *chi*; and choose house plants that do not have sharp leaves—they can also disrupt *chi*.

91 Magnet chill

For years, doctors have derided magnet therapy as sheer quackery. Yet recent research has led to a gradual acceptance that it might have some value in certain circumstances. Stress is one of these—so, when you're tense, it may help if you try a magnet chill. One theory is that magnetic fields act on acupoints to balance your flow of life energy. There's a huge number of magnetic products on the market for various conditions—you can buy magnetic trainers, insoles, necklaces, and pads, to name a few. However, if you're stressed, a magnetic bracelet, which acts on acupoints in the wrist, may be all you need.

92 Tree chill

Trees can help you chill? People have thought so for thousands of years. Think of the oak, ash, and mistletoe of Celtic druids, and of the "personal trees" of Native Americans. There's a legendary acceptance that trees harbor mysterious energies that can both ground you and inspire you. Choose a strong vibrant tree with slim, flexible branches. Gently tie one of its twigs into a knot. Then visualize your stress pouring into it. Sense the stress leaving your body. Then carefully untie the knot to sever your link with the tree, so that the negative energy can be neutralized.

93 Solar chill

According to the ancient Vedic texts of the Hindu religion, the sun is the storehouse of inexhaustible power and the sustainer of all life. And in every energy-based belief system, the sun is seen as a source of health-giving positive energy. But how can you make use of it? With a solar chill. It's as simple as sun-bathing. Just strip down on a hot summer's day and soak up the warmth of the rays, feeling their positive energy diluting your stress. But make sure that you use a good sunscreen——it will deflect the harmful ultraviolet light, but not the beneficial energy.

94 Remedy chill

Homeopathy has had a mixed press lately. Opponents say that the active substances are diluted so much that no chemical trace of them remains; supporters believe that the substances leave behind "imprints" of energy that trigger the body's vital force to start self-healing. Whatever sceptics say, thousands of people find that homeopathy works for them. If you've never tried it, why not join them and try a remedy chill when you're anxious and tense? For preference, consult a qualified homeopath, but otherwise try Aconite 6c—it's the homeopathic remedy for shock, emotional stress, and panic attacks.

95 Sun and moon chill

As "life force" energy is believed to move through space as well as your body, it can be breathed in and out. That means that the negative energy of stress, symbolized by the moon, can be breathed away, and the positive energy of the sun breathed in—and that's what you do in a sun and moon chill. Sit up with a straight back, gently pinch your nostrils shut, and breathe through your mouth. Then breathe in through your right nostril, hold the breath, and then exhale through your left nostril. Repeat five times. Then switch nostrils for five more breaths.

96 T'ai chi chill

Also called "meditation in motion," T'ai chi is an ancient Chinese technique that applies Taoist philosophical principles to the art of movement to influence *chi,* the body's life energy. A study of 1992 showed that it's an effective way of relieving stress, which wasn't news to the millions of Chinese who perform T'ai chi's graceful, flowing movements as a daily ritual. Enroll in a class, but choose one that emphasizes the art's healing side rather than its martial aspects. You'll be able to T'ai chi chill whenever you like.

97 Pyramid chill

Egypt's Great Pyramid of Cheops, more than 4,500 years old, has a unique shape and set of proportions. And research has shown that its shape concentrates the earth's electromagnetic waves in ways that we still don't understand. Over the years, many claims have been made for the power of pyramids, from relieving stress and affecting mood to keeping razor blades sharp. Whatever their truth, many people swear by the relaxing and invigorating power of a pyramid. Buy one from a health store and join them—hang it over your bed or a favorite chair, and take a pyramid chill.

98 Cry chill

Everybody feels better after a good cry. But you don't necessarily feel better if you're crying from pain or because you've been peeling onions. But why? Scientists have discovered that the tears you cry through emotion are very different to those that you cry for other reasons. They contain around 25 percent more protein, and a range of chemicals, including hormones. This has led some therapists to speculate that crying through emotion is a way of discarding negative energy. So don't hang on to negative feelings—release all that emotional stress, and have a cry chill.

99 Reiki chill

In the late 19th century, a Japanese monk rediscovered the chants used to summon the Medicine Buddha in ancient Tibet and reformulated the art of reiki as a spiritual healing system. It's becoming increasingly popular in the West—and is claimed to be a particularly effective stress buster. Unfortunately, it's not a DIY chill, and you need to consult a reiki practitioner. The idea is that the practitioner's "reiki energy" is channelled through his or her hands into your body to dissolve the energy blockages caused by stress. It's said to be strangely relaxing yet invigorating.

100 Prayer chill

All over the world, millions use the power of prayer to relieve their stress, rather than resort to any alternative therapies. It's not surprising, because spirituality is the most powerful energy of them all. And prayer draws not only on spirituality, but also on the healing properties of meditation. So when you're stressed out and life problems are getting on top of you, find a quiet place in which to pray to your god. Move unhurriedly through the four phases of supplication, meditation, appreciation, and application. The power of prayer should never be underestimated.

acknowledgments

Cover photograph ©Konrad Wothe/Image State

note

This book is not intended to be a guide to the medical treatment of stress. If you suffer from persistent or severe stress, or think that you may have a stress-related disorder, consult your physician. You should also check with your physician before undertaking any new exercise regime, and before taking any herbal preparation if you are pregnant, trying to become pregnant, breastfeeding, or taking any prescribed medication.